I0484723

Marketing Management

:: Author ::

Hetal Parmar

(M.COM., M.phil., SLET)

PUBLISHED BY

Hemchadracharya International Publishing House
HQ. At & Po. Chaveli., Ta- Chansma,
Dist- Patan, North Gujarat, India, Asia.
www.iphouseindia.com

First Publication: 26TH January, 2015

Copyright: Author
(c) Hetal Parmar

ISBN:- 978-15-08712-16-9

Price: Rs.750/- INDIA
$ 15 OUTSIDE INDIA

PUBLISHED BY

Hemchadracharya International Publishing House
HQ. At & Po. Chaveli., Ta- Chansma,
Dist- Patan, North Gujarat, India, Asia.
www.iphouseindia.com

Contents

Sr.no	Particulars	Page no.
Unit 1	(A) Marketing – An Introduction	01
	(B) Marketing Mix and Marketing concept	20
Unit 2	(A) Branding	34
	(B) Pricing	48
	(C) Advertising	64
Unit 3	Consumer Behaviour and Market Segmentation	
	(A) Consumer Behaviour	74
	(B) Market Segmentation	94
Unit 4	Marketing Research	104

Unit – 01

(A) Marketing – An Introduction

1.1 Definition of marketing

Marketing is the science of meeting the needs of a customer by providing valuable products to customers by utilizing the expertise of the organization, at same time, to achieve organizational goals. According to The American Marketing Association [1]:

Marketing is the activity, set of institutions, and processes for creating, communicating, delivering, and exchanging offerings that have value for customers, clients, partners, and society at large.

With this definition, it is important to realize that the customer can be an individual user, a company, or several people who contribute to the purchasing decision. The product can be a hard good, a service, or even an idea – anything that would provide some value to the person who provides an exchange. An exchange is most often thought of as money, but could also be a donation of time or effort, or even a specific action. A producer is often a company, but could be an individual or non-profit organization.

Classical marketing is often described in terms of the four "P's, which are:

- **Product** – what goods or services are offered to customers

- **Promotion** – how the producer communicates the value of its products

- **Price** – the value of the exchange between the customer and producer

- **Placement** – how the product is delivered to the customer.

A complete analysis of these categories is often called the **Marketing Mix**. More detail on these categories can be found in the later entry on the Marketing Plan.

Marketing has both inbound and outbound activities. Inbound activities largely center on discovering the needs and wants of the potential customers. The collective group of all potential customers is called a market. Categorizing these needs into groups is called segmentation. Organizing markets into segments allows a producer to more logically decide how to best provide value to that group of potential customers. The analysis of market segment needs; analysis of existing sales and profitability; the descriptions, design and introduction of new products; and the analysis of competitor offerings are also inbound activities that are important but not often seen by the public.

Outbound activities include all aspects of informing the market that a product is available, delivering that product, and encouraging the purchase decision. These activities include advertising, promotion, supply chain, sales support, product training, and customer support.

To the public, the most common interaction with marketing is where it touches the discipline of sales in the form of advertising. This interaction leads to a common misconception that marketing is only this aspect of promotion. Instead, it is useful in understanding that:

Marketing management is the art and science of choosing target markets and getting, keeping, and growing customers through creating, delivering, and communicating superior customer value.

MARKEITNG MIX

PRICE

Types of Pricing:

- ▣ Premium Pricing
- ▣ Penetration Pricing
- ▣ Economy Pricing
- ▣ Price Skimming
- ▣ Psychological Pricing
- ▣ Product Line Pricing
- ▣ Optional Product Pricing
- ▣ Captive Product Pricing
- ▣ Product Bundle Pricing

- Promotional Pricing
- Geographical Pricing
- Value Pricing

PLACE

Types of Channel Intermediaries are as follows.

- Wholesalers
- Agents
- Retailers
- Internet

PRODUCT

PROMOTION

The elements of the promotions mix are:

- Personal Selling.
- Sales Promotion.

- ◙ Public Relations.

- ◙ Direct Mail.

- ◙ Trade Fairs and Exhibitions.

- ◙ Advertising.

- ◙ Sponsorship.

PRICING OBJECTIVES

- ◙ Partial cost recovery

- ◙ Profit margin maximization

- ◙ Profit maximization

- ◙ Revenue maximization

- ◙ Quality leadership

- ◙ Quantity maximization

- ◙ Status quo

- ◙ Survival

1.2 Characteristics of Marketing

◙ **1. Marketing is an integrated process**- Marketing is not a single activity. It is rather a coordination of several inter-related activities. The interaction between different activities gives a unique character to marketing. Marketing is a managerial process in so far as it involves the functions of planning and control. Marketing is also a social process as it is concerned with the satisfaction of human needs and this is one of the most important Characteristics of Marketing.

▣ **2. Marketing is customer oriented**- Marketing exists to identify and satisfy the wants of present and potential consumers. Customer is the focus of all marketing activities.

▣ **3. Marketing is a system**- Another important characteristic of marketing is its function as a system. Marketing is a system comprising several sub systems. Under marketing inputs are drawn from the society and converted into outputs which are supplied to the society.

▣ **4. Marketing is a part of total environment**- Marketing operates within the framework of total environment which comprises economic, social, legal, political, international and other forces. Changes in the environment influence marketing activities. Marketing is, therefore, a dynamic process as it keeps on adjusting to the changing environment.

▣ **5. Marketing is creative**- Marketing creates time, place and possession utilities. Time utility is created by preserving goods for use in future. Place utility is created by carrying goods to places where they are needed the most. Marketing creates possession utility by transferring products and services from producer to customer. Exchange process between buyer and seller is the essential element in marketing.

◙ 6. **Marketing is goal -oriented**- Of the many important characteristics of marketing; one very important aspect is it is goal-oriented. Marketing seeks to achieve benefits, for both buyer and seller. It results in mutually beneficial relationship by satisfying wants of customers and by generating revenues for customers.

◙ 7. **Marketing is pervasive**- marketing is required in business as well in social and other organizations. In other organizations, marketing is necessary for spreading socially useful ideas and programs family planning, adult education, communal harmony, national integration, environmental protection, etc. Such marketing is called social marketing.

◙ So these are the important Characteristics of Marketing without which marketing can't be successful. The traditional marketing concept has lost it value and the

Characteristics of Marketing revolves around the modern approach to marketing.

1.3 Importance of Marketing Management:

Marketing management has gained importance to meet increasing competition and the need for improved methods of distribution to reduce cost and to increase profits. Marketing management today is the most important function in a commercial and business enterprise.

The following are the other factors showing importance of the marketing management:

(i) Introduction of new products in the market.

(ii) Increasing the production of existing products.

(iii) Reducing cost of sales and distribution.

(iv) Export market.

(v) Development in the means of communication and modes of transportation within and outside the country.

(vi) Rise in per capita income and demand for more goods by the consumers.

1.4 Functions of Marketing

1. Selling:

It is core of marketing. It is concerned with the prospective buyers to actually complete the purchase of an article. It involves transfer of ownership of goods to the buyer. Selling plays an important part in realising the ultimate aim of earring profit. Selling is enhanced by means of personal selling, advertising, publicity and sales promotion. Effectiveness and efficiency in selling determines the volume of company's profits and profitability.

2. Buying and Assembling:

It involves what to buy, of what quality, how much from whom, when and at what price. People in business buy to increase sales or to decrease costs. Purchasing agents are much influenced by quality, service and price.

The products that the retailers buy for resale are determined by the needs and preferences of their customers. A manufacturer buys raw materials, spare parts, machinery, equipment's, etc. for carrying out his production process and other related activities. A Wholesaler buys products to resell them to the retailers.

Assembling means to purchase necessary component parts and to fit them together to make a product. 'Assembly line' indicates a production line made up of purely assembly operations. The assembly operation involves the arrival of individual component parts at the work place and issuing of these parts to be fastened together in the form of an assembly or sub-assembly.

Assembly line is an arrangement of workers and machines in which each person has a particular job and the work is passed directly from one worker to the next until the product is complete. On the other hand, 'fabrication lines' implies a production line made up of operations that form or change the physical or sometimes chemical characteristics of the product involved.

3. Transportation:

Transportation is the physical means by which goods are moved from the places where they are produced to those places where they are needed for consumption. It creates place, utility. Transportation is essential from the procurement of raw material to the delivery of finished products to the customer's places. Marketing relies mainly on railroads, trucks, waterways, pipelines and air transport.

The type of transportation is chosen on several considerations, such as suitability, speed and cost. Transportation may be performed either by the buyer or by the seller. The nature and kind of the transportation facilities determine the extent of the marketing area, the regularity in supply, uniform price maintenance and easy access to the supplier or seller.

4. Storage:

It involves holding of goods in proper (i.e., usable or saleable) condition from the time they are produced until they are needed by customers (in case of finished products) or by the production department (in case of raw materials and stores); storing protects the goods from deterioration and helps in carrying over surplus for future consumption or use in production.

Goods may be stored in various warehouses situated at different places, which is popularly known as warehousing. Warehouses should be situated at such places from where the distribution of goods may be easier and cheaper. Situation of warehouses is also important from the view of prompt feeding of emergency demands. Storing assumes importance when production is regional or consumption may be regional. Retail firms are called "stores".

5. Standardization and Grading:

The other activities that facilitate marketing are standardisation and grading. Standardisation means establishment of certain standards or specifications for products based on intrinsic physical qualities of any commodity.

This may involve quantity (weight or size) or it may involve quality (colour, shape, appearance, material, taste, sweetness etc.) Government may also set some standards, for example, in case of agricultural products. A standard conveys a uniformity of the products.

Grading means classification of standardised products into certain well defined classes or groups. It involves the division of products into classes made of units possessing similar characteristics of size and quality. Grading is very important for raw materials, marketing of agricultural products (such as fruits and cereals), mining products (such as coal, iron and manganese) and forest products (such as timber). Branded consumer products may bear grade labels A, B, C.

6. Financing:

It involves the use of capital to meet financial requirements of agencies dealing with various activities of marketing. The services to provide the credit and money needed, the costs of getting merchandise into the hands of the final user is commonly referred to as finanace function in marketing.

In marketing, finances are needed for working capital and fixed capital which may be secured from three sources—owned capital, bank loans and advance and trade credit. (Provided by manufacturers to wholesaler and by the wholesaler to the retailers.) In other words; various kinds of finances are short-term finance, medium-term finance, and long-term finance.

7. Risk Taking:

Risk means loss due to some unforeseen circumstances in future. Risk bearing in marketing refers to the financial risk interest in the ownership of goods held for an anticipated demand including the possible losses due to a fall in prices and the losses from spoilage, depreciation, obsolescence, fire and floods or any other loss that may occur with the passage of time.

From production of goods to its selling stage, many risks are involved due to changes in market conditions, natural causes and human factors. Changes in fashion or inventions also cause risks. Legislative measures of government may also cause risks. Risks may arise during the course of transportation.

They may also be due to decay, deterioration and accidents, or due to fluctuation in the prices caused by changes in their supply and demand. The various risks are usually termed as place risk, time risk and physical risk, etc.

8. Market Information:

The importance of this facilitating function of marketing has been recognised only recently. The only sound foundation on which marketing decisions may be based is correct and timely market information. Right facts and information reduce the aforesaid risks and thereby result in cost reduction.

Modern marketing requires a lot of information adequately, accurately and speedily. Marketing information makes a seller know when to sell, at what price to sell, who are the competitors, etc. Marketing information and its proper analysis has led to marketing research which has now become an independent branch of marketing.

Business firms collect, analyse and interpret facts and information from internal sources, such as records, sales-people and findings of the market research department. They also seek facts and information from external sources, such as business publications, government reports and commercial research firms.

Retailers need to know about sources of supply and also about customers "buying motives and buying habits". Manufacturers need to know about retailers and about advertising media. Firms in both these groups need information about 'competitor' activities and about their markets.

Even ultimate consumers need market information about availability of products, their quality standards, their prices and also about the after sale service facility. Common sources for consumers are sales people, media advertisements, colleagues, etc.

1.5 DIFFERENCE BETWEEN SELLING AND MARKETING

In general we use 'marketing' and 'selling' as synonyms but there is a substantial difference between both the concepts. It is necessary to understand the differences between Marketing vs Selling for a successful marketing manager. Selling has a product focus and mostly producer driven. It is the action part of marketing only and has short – term goal of achieving market share. The emphasis is on price variation for closing the sale where the objective can be stated, as "I must somehow sell the product". This short – term focus does not consider a prudential planning for building up the brand in the market place and winning competitive advantage through a high loyal set of customers. The end means of any sales activity is maximizing profits through sales maximization.

When the focus is on selling, the businessman thinks that after production has been completed the task of the sales force starts. It is also the task of the sales department to sell whatever the production department has manufactured. Aggressive sales methods are justified to meet this goal and customer's actual needs and satisfaction are taken for granted. Selling converts the product in to cash for the company in the short run.

Marketing as a concept and approach is much wider than selling and is also dynamic as the focus is on the customer rather than the product. While selling revolves around the needs and interest of the manufacturer or marketer, marketing revolves around that of consumer. It is the whole process of meeting and satisfying the needs of the consumer.

Marketing consists of all those activities that are associated with product planning, pricing, promoting and distributing the product or service. The task commences with identifying consumer needs and does not end till feedback on consumer sat-is faction from the consumption of the product is received. It is a long chain of activity, which comprises production, packing, promotion, pricing, distribution and then the selling. Consumer needs become the guiding force behind all these activities. Profits are not ignored but they are built up on a long run basis. Mind share is more important than market share in Marketing.

	Marketing	**Sales**
Approach	Broader range of activities to sell product/service, client relationship etc.; determine future needs and has a strategy in place to meet those needs for the long term relationship.	Makes customer demand match the products the company currently offers.
Focus	Overall picture to promote, distribute, price products/services; fulfill	fulfill sales volume objectives

	customer's wants and needs through products and/or services the company can offer.	
Process	Analysis of market, distribution channels, competitive products and services; Pricing strategies; Sales tracking and market share analysis; Budget	Usually one to one
Scope	Market research; Advertising; Sales; Public relations; Customer service and satisfaction .	Once a product has been created for a customer need, persuade the customer to purchase the product to fulfill her needs
Priority	Marketing shows how to reach to the Customers and build long lasting	Selling is the ultimate result of marketing.

	relationship	
Identity	Marketing targets the construction of a brand identity so that it becomes easily associated with need fulfillment.	Sales is the strategy of meeting needs in an opportunistic, individual method, driven by human interaction. There's no premise of brand identity, longevity or continuity. It's simply the ability to meet a need at the right time.
Horizon	Longer term	Short term

(B) **Marketing Mix and Marketing concept**

1.6 Definition of 'Marketing Mix'

Definition: The marketing mix refers to the set of actions, or tactics, that a company uses to promote its brand or product in the market. The 4Ps make up a typical marketing mix - Price, Product, Promotion and Place. However, nowadays, the marketing mix increasingly includes several other Ps like Packaging, Positioning, People and even Politics as vital mix elements.

1.7 Description: What are the 4Ps of marketing?

Price: refers to the value that is put for a product. It depends on costs of production, segment targeted, ability of the market to pay, supply - demand and a host of other direct and indirect factors. There can be several types of pricing strategies, each tied in with an overall business plan. Pricing can also be used a demarcation, to differentiate and enhance the image of a product.

Product: refers to the item actually being sold. The product must deliver a minimum level of performance; otherwise even the best work on the other elements of the marketing mix won't do any good.

Place: refers to the point of sale. In every industry, catching the eye of the consumer and making it easy for her to buy it is the main aim of a good distribution or 'place' strategy. Retailers pay a premium for the right location. In fact, the mantra of a successful retail business is 'location, location, location'.

Promotion: this refers to all the activities undertaken to make the product or service known to the user and trade. This can include advertising, word of mouth, press reports, incentives, commissions and awards to the trade. It can also include consumer schemes, direct marketing, contests and prizes.

Product

The product is either a tangible good or an intangible service that is seem to meet a specific customer need or demand. All products follow a logical product life cycle and it is vital for marketers to understand and plan for the various stages and their unique challenges. It is key to understand those problems that the product is attempting to solve. The benefits offered by the product and all its features need to be understood and the unique selling proposition of the product need to be studied. In addition, the potential buyers of the product need to be identified and understood.

Price

Price covers the actual amount the end user is expected to pay for a product. How a product is priced will directly affect how it sells. This is linked to what the perceived value of the product is to the customer rather than an objective costing of the product on offer. If a product is priced higher or lower than its perceived value, then it will not sell. This is why it is imperative to understand how a customer sees what you are selling. If there is a positive customer value, than a product may be successfully priced higher than its objective monetary value. Conversely, if a product has little value in the eyes of the consumer, then it may need to be underpriced to sell. Price may also be affected by distribution plans, value chain costs and markups and how competitors price a rival product.

Promotion

The marketing communication strategies and techniques all fall under the promotion heading. These may include advertising, sales promotions, special offers and public relations. Whatever the channel used, it is necessary for it to be suitable for the product, the price and the end user it is being marketed to. It is important to differentiate between marketing and promotion. Promotion is just the communication aspect of the entire marketing function.

Place

Place or placement has to do with how the product will be provided to the customer. Distribution is a key element of placement. The placement strategy will help assess what channel is the most suited to a product. How a product is accessed by the end user also needs to compliment the rest of the product strategy.

1.8 approach: *'Marketing Mix'*

- Designs the modeling methodology to better capture marketing impact on more complex B2B and B2C sales

- Provides interpretative analyses and action plans designed around increasing immediate performance while also making efforts to improve under-performing channels

- Brings our deep financial expertise to support ROI calculations ranging from initial purchase to customer lifetime value

- Integrates modeling into a more comprehensive measurement plan to further maximize performance over the long-term

- Offers the option to leverage the results into our advanced marketing ROI scenario planning tools to guide marketing mix plan development

- **The Five Concepts Described**

- **The Production Concept.** This concept is the oldest of the concepts in business. It holds that consumers will prefer products that are widely available and inexpensive. Managers focusing on this concept concentrate on achieving high production efficiency, low costs, and mass distribution. They assume that consumers are primarily interested in product availability and low prices. This orientation makes sense in developing countries, where consumers are more interested in obtaining the product than in its features.

- **The Product Concept.** This orientation holds that consumers will favor those products that offer the most quality, performance, or innovative features. Managers focusing on this concept concentrate on making superior products and improving them over time. They assume that buyers admire well-made products and can appraise quality and performance. However, these managers are sometimes caught up in a love affair with their product and do not realize what the market needs. Management might commit the "better-mousetrap" fallacy, believing that a better mousetrap will lead people to beat a path to its door.

- **The Selling Concept.** This is another common business orientation. It holds that consumers and businesses, if left alone, will ordinarily not buy enough of the selling company's products. The organization must, therefore, undertake an aggressive selling and promotion effort. This concept assumes that consumers typically sho9w buyi8ng inertia or resistance and must be coaxed into buying. It also assumes that the company has a whole battery of effective selling and promotional tools to stimulate more buying. Most firms practice the selling concept when they have overcapacity. *Their aim is to* sell *what they make rather than make what the market wants.*

- **The Marketing Concept.** This is a business philosophy that challenges the above three business orientations. Its central tenets crystallized in the 1950s. It holds that the key to achieving its organizational goals (goals of the selling company) consists of the company being more effective than competitors in creating, delivering, and communicating customer value to its selected target customers. The marketing concept rests on four pillars: target market, customer needs, integrated marketing and profitability.

1.9 Distinctions between the Sales Concept and the Marketing Concept:

1. The Sales Concept focuses on the needs of the seller. The Marketing Concept focuses on the needs of the buyer.

2. The Sales Concept is preoccupied with the seller's need to convert his/her product into cash. The Marketing Concept is preoccupied with the idea of satisfying the needs of the customer by means of the product as a solution to the customer's problem (needs).

   - The Marketing Concept represents the major change in today's company orientation that provides the foundation to achieve *competitive advantage*. This philosophy is the foundation of *consultative selling*.

   - The Marketing Concept has evolved into a fifth and more refined company orientation: The Societal Marketing Concept. This concept is more theoretical and will undoubtedly influence future forms of marketing and selling approaches.

1. **Production Concept**

   - Those companies who believe in this philosophy think that if the goods/services are cheap and they can be made available at many places, there cannot be any problem regarding sale.

- Keeping in mind the same philosophy these companies put in all their marketing efforts in reducing the cost of production and strengthening their distribution system. In order to reduce the cost of production and to bring it down to the minimum level, these companies indulge in large scale production.

- This helps them in effecting the economics of the large scale production. Consequently, the cost of production per unit is reduced.

- The utility of this philosophy is apparent only when demand exceeds supply. Its greatest drawback is that it is not always necessary that the customer every time purchases the cheap and easily available goods or services.

2. Product Concept

Those companies who believe in this philosophy are of the opinion that if the quality of goods or services is of good standard, the customers can be easily attracted. The basis of this thinking is that the customers get attracted towards the products of good quality. On the basis of this philosophy or idea these companies direct their marketing efforts to increasing the quality of their product.

- It is a firm belief of the followers of the product concept that the customers get attracted to the products of good quality. This is not the absolute truth because it is not the only basis of buying goods.

- The customers do take care of the price of the products, its availability, etc. A good quality product and high price can upset the budget of a customer. Therefore, it can be said that only the quality of the product is not the only way to the success of marketing.

3. Selling Concept

Those companies who believe in this concept think that leaving alone the customers will not help. Instead there is a need to attract the customers towards them. They think that goods are not bought but they have to be sold.

- The basis of this thinking is that the customers can be attracted. Keeping in view this concept these companies concentrate their marketing efforts towards educating and attracting the customers. In such a case their main thinking is 'selling what you have'.

- This concept offers the idea that by repeated efforts one can sell-anything to the customers. This may be right for some time, but you cannot do it for a long-time. If you succeed in enticing the customer once, he cannot be won over every time.

- On the contrary, he will work for damaging your reputation. Therefore, it can be asserted that this philosophy offers only a short-term advantage and is not for long-term gains.

4. Marketing Concept

Those companies who believe in this concept are of the opinion that success can be achieved only through consumer satisfaction. The basis of this thinking is that only those goods/service should be made available which the consumers want or desire and not the things which you can do.

- In other words, they do not sell what they can make but they make what they can sell. Keeping in mind this idea, these companies direct their marketing efforts to achieve consumer satisfaction.

- In short, it can be said that it is a modern concept and by adopting it profit can be earned on a long-term basis. The drawback of this concept is that no attention is paid to social welfare.

5. Societal Marketing Concept

This concept stresses not only the customer satisfaction but also gives importance to Consumer Welfare/Societal Welfare. This concept is almost a step further than the marketing concept. Under this concept, it is believed that mere satisfaction of the consumers would not help and the welfare of the whole society has to be kept in mind.

- For example, if a company produces a vehicle which consumes less petrol but spreads pollution, it will result in only consumer satisfaction and not the social welfare.

- Primarily two elements are included under social welfare-high-level of human life and pollution free atmosphere. Therefore, the companies believing in this concept direct all their marketing efforts towards the achievement of consumer satisfaction and social welfare.

- In short, it can be said that this is the latest concept of marketing. The companies adopting this concept can achieve long-term profit.

- **The Societal Marketing Concept.** This concept holds that the organization's task is to determine the needs, wants, and interests of target markets and to deliver the desired satisfactions more effectively and efficiently than competitors (this is the original Marketing Concept). Additionally, it holds that this all must be done in a way that preserves or enhances the consumer's and the society's well-being.

- This orientation arose as some questioned whether the Marketing Concept is an appropriate philosophy in an age of environmental deterioration, resource shortages, explosive population growth, world hunger and poverty, and neglected social services.

- Are companies that do an excellent job of satisfying consumer wants necessarily acting in the best long-run interests of consumers and society?

- The marketing concept possibily sidesteps the potential conflicts among consumer wants, consumer interests, and long-run societal welfare. Just consider:

- The fast-food hamburger industry offers tasty buty unhealthy food. The hamburgers have a high fat content, and the restaurants promote fries and pies, two products high in starch and fat. The products are wrapped in convenient packaging, which leads to much waste. In satisfying consumer wants, these restaurants may be hurting consumer health and causing environmental problems.

Unit – 02

(A)BRANDING

The process involved in creating a unique name and image for a product in the consumers' mind, mainly through advertising campaigns with a consistent theme.

Branding aims to establish a significant and Differentiated presence in the marketthat attracts and retains loyal customers.

2.3 Types of branding

Product

Products enjoy some of the most common types of branding. Walking through supermarket or retail store aisles is an easy way to understand product branding. Certain labels will jump off the shelves because they have achieved their marketing goals. Successful product branding is what nudges a consumer to choose one brand over another. The brand has established a reputation as the best or most popular in its class. Think of soft drinks, athletic shoes, computers or jeans and see what brand names pop into your head first. These are prime examples of product branding.

Personal

Personal branding is a popular marketing tool among athletes, musicians, politicians and other celebrities. A politician will attempt to brand himself into the type of person the voters want to put in office. A celebrity often becomes self-branded based on his own personality, while others are molded by public relations firms and agents. In addition to a personal brand, a celebrity might become associated with products bearing his name.

Corporate

Corporate branding is essential for any business that wants to develop a reputation in the marketplace. Everything the company does has an effect on its image. A corporation markets its product or service, its corporate culture, its employees and its contributions to the community. A corporation's branding can become tarnished overnight because of an industrial disaster or a poor decision by management. If the damage is severe, a corporation might start over with an entirely new strategy for branding a completely new image.

Geographic

Geographic or regional branding conjures images of certain products or services when the name is mentioned. While the Southwest region of the U.S. might be known for spicy foods, the Midwest is known for steaks. The tourism industry uses branding to lure travelers to the area. Southern states boast their sunshine and beaches, while mountainous areas become known for winter sports such as skiing and snowboarding.

Cultural

Cultural branding develops a reputation about the environment and people of a particular location or nationality. New Englanders are thought to be hard-working, and perhaps too serious, while New Yorkers are viewed as people always on the go and moving at a rapid-fire pace. Cultural branding is another tool in tourism such as inviting travelers to experience the Amish country.

2.4 The importance of brand

Uniqueness

Utilize your branding to set yourself apart from your competitors. To do this, analyze what you do best and consider you target demographic. Use graphics and word choices that clearly reflect your business to your target audience, hence your brand. Use your branding to deliver clear messages.

Target Audience

Done correctly, your brand can assist you in getting a stronger foothold in your niche market. Define your unique selling position and consider methods to communicate key messages to your desired audience. Use specific images or phrases to encourage the feel of inclusivity. Let them know the reason your company exists and how it can fulfill their needs. This can connect you to your target audience, engage them and motivate them to buy.

Related Reading: Corporate Branding vs. Product Branding

Emotional Connections

According to a 2010 study conducted by the world's largest public relations firm, Edelman, the Y Generation, also known as the Millennials, consider brand identification almost as important as religious preference and ethnic background when defining themselves online. The power of branding has successfully melded into that of personal identification and emotional connection.

Message Delivery

Having strong branding can evoke trust from your niche market. This can translate to your newsletters, emails and advertisements garnering a greater response, hence increasing sales. As people will already be vested in your brand, they will be confident that they will receive value for time spent reading your messages or researching your product.

Consistency

Focus on your long-term branding efforts to keep your business consistent. This consistency should transcend messages, product lines and audience appeal. It should enhance your business, adding depth to your company's presence. This should allow you to grow and keep a loyal following.

2.5 The Disadvantages of Brand Identity

Complex

The brand identity building process is complex. This is especially true for organizations that offer a range of services and products. The process entails extensive research, including market research, marketing audit, competitive audit and usability, and a clear branding strategy. Furthermore, a brand identity is only truly successful when customers closely identify with the brand. This happens when a brand caters to customer requirements and preferences. Marketers have to keep this in mind and ensure that the brand identity is aligned with, and relevant to, its customers.

Expensive to Design

Designing and creating a brand identity is expensive and time consuming. Brands either delegate the task to their marketing teams or hire consultants who charge by the hour and spend many hours in close consultation with managers before they decide on the brand logotype, color, typography, sound, motion and other key elements of the brand identity design. Trial applications are run before the identity is presented for approval. The approved identity is then trademarked and translated to the company website, business cards, letterheads, packaging and advertising. Each step of the process entails heavy funding and expenses.

Related Reading: The Key Components to a New Brand Identity

Difficult to Maintain

It is not always easy for companies to maintain brand identity. This is because of changing customer preferences, product or service diversification or company expansion.

Marketers must choose marketing channels carefully so as to not tarnish the brand identity. For example, a company that manufactures top-of-the-line electronic equipment may hurt its brand identity by renting out shelf space in a discount or bargain store. This also makes sustaining brand identity difficult.

Difficult and Expensive to Change

Changing and modifying brand identity is difficult and entails extensive planning and managerial skills. Managers responsible for the change are required to possess sound public relations, branding, communications, productions, marketing and management expertise. Information about the change must be conveyed to customers and other stakeholders. Change often is met with resistance and a brand may lose valuable customers. Furthermore, changing brand identity is expensive as it directly affects numerous applications and each needs to be subsequently changed, including business cards, stationery, forms, marketing materials, websites, directory listings, name tags, uniforms and signage.

2.6 Essential of good branding

1. **Single-minded** – a brand essence must rely on just one absorbing thing to say about the brand otherwise it will lack focus.

   It's not written to pamper the clients desire for a list of apparently inadmissible features.

2. **Unique** – we notice what is different about something; not what is the same. At the heart of a strong brand is how it is different from competitors.

   We don't buy a dress because everyone at work is wearing it.

3. **Experiential** – a brand essence captures what the consumer feels during an experience with the brand.

   It's a consumer's definition; its not internal jargon.

4. **Relevant** – the essence must be relevant to the consumer – a brand's essence must be desirable and vital.

   It's what matters to them; not what you say it is.

5. **Consistently delivered** – If the core audience doesn't consistently experience it then practically it isn't the true essence.

   The character of a brand must be consistently represented across all company operations and marketing mediums.

6. **Authentic** – the brand essence must be believable or the brand will be rejected. Its allowed to be aspirational as long as

the consumer believes you can deliver on the promise. *Consumers expect the truth and the real thing from brand owners.*

7. **Durable** – the brand essence will stand over time. It doesn't change.Ever.

Logos may come and go, packaging may change but the brand essence remains.

1. Pitch

Every business needs a pitch. Your pitch is the source of your business personality. It should be clear, confident and strike up a connection with your audience in a few sparse words. Whether you are using it to entice investors or customers these phrases should instantly convey the spark behind your brand.

How would you sum up your business in a nutshell? Think about what makes you unique, what you offer your customers and the driving principles behind your business.

If you can define your story in just a few words or sentences then you are on your way to creating a strong brand. For a brilliant step by step process on creating a concise and versatile 100-200 word pitch for your business this article is brilliant: So, What Do You Do? How to Craft the Perfect Pitch.

2. Voice

Beyond the carefully selected wording of your pitch there is a whole world of copy that will need to be written for and about your business. From web pages to product descriptions to social media posts, it is vital to make sure all communications are created using a well defined personality that will keep the tone and language consistent.

Without a clear "voice" to use copy is subject to change, reflecting the various personalities and moods of each writer. Defining a tone of voice for your brand that is designed to resonate with your target audience will keep all copy authentic, regardless of when or where it is used or who writes it. Consistency will give your voice strength.

3. Logo Design

Think of your pitch as the way your brand introduces itself and your voice as the conversation that follows. Your logo design is the visual representation of the two, and is often the most memorable aspect of your brand. It should complement and strengthen your branding, creating a firm and instant impression of your business.

There are a number of key components that make up a good logo design, one of which is colour. There are well established guidelines for which colours to use in a logo, with blue generally invoking a sense of trust, purple conveying imagination and creativity, and orange reflecting an almost whimsical playfulness.

Choose your logo carefully and make sure it is fit for purpose and well designed.

For more information on how to ensure your logo is effectively representing your brand check out this article: The 4 Fundamentals of a Good Logo Design.

4. Be the Expert

Once you have defined the story, look and personality of your brand it is time to bring it all to life. The key to doing this well is to stay focused. Build an authentic presence in your niche by establishing your authority, and continuing to be a consistent and confident player in that space.

Think about the demographics of your audience in order to offer them advice, products or services that speak to their needs and relate to their problems.

Branding is something that requires ongoing curation, and sometimes evolution as your target audience and business offerings change, but lay your foundations right and you will have a core brand philosophy and image to build on as your business develops.

1. A badly managed brand implementation is like a bottomless money pit.

Before you start, an analysis of the visual, organizational, and financial impacts of the implementation is essential. Incorporate centralized tracking of all costs to ensure that there are no nasty surprises, for you or the stakeholders.

2. Project planning is crucial.

Given the scale of work, it is necessary to prioritize where and how efforts should be concentrated in order to ensure individual business units know exactly how to approach rebranding. Realistic targets, backed by practical and technical knowledge, need to be set in order to push the brand implementation through.

3. Extraordinary levels of detailed information are gathered in order to build an effective implementation plan.

This information is priceless – uploaded onto an online project management system it can help protect your investment and provide an ongoing point of reference for existing and future stakeholders.

4. The design stage is the least expensive but most glamorous aspect of a (re)branding process.

As a result it receives the most attention from senior management despite the fact that the real challenge, and cost, comes down to implementation. In our experience, the ratio between the expenditures for branding consultants and design compared to the cost for implementation could be 1:20, depending on the size and complexity of the organization. Momentum is easily lost when the sheer scale of work required becomes apparent; therefore, it is vital that senior management remain involved right up until the last sign is installed. Otherwise, the program will lose focus.

5. The integrity of the design must be protected by implementing a consistent and manageable image.

Impractical designs are harder and more expensive to implement, so the design stage must be guided by practical advice. Don't forget to set up a thorough design briefing, which includes aesthetic, communicative, technical and legal requirements.

6. Translate the basic design to designs for different brand touch points like signage, vehicles, stationery, and clothing.

Make prototypes before the real implementation. What looks good on a piece of paper may not look the same on top of a 20-story building.

7. Global brands require global implementation management.

A lot of brand touch points will involve multiple regional suppliers, even if modular designs are manufactured centrally. Partnering with an international implementation agency will promote consistency and cost control.

8. Obtaining the buy-in of local managers to your branding program and reducing the possibility of local maverick activity diluting the brand is crucial.

Local teams must understand the reason behind the (re)branding and how a consistent image will benefit them directly. Acceptance of brand standards is not automatic. Most people see their department's or unit's circumstances as an exception – do not give them any excuses; instead give the support required to get the job done.

9. Emphasize internal communication about the project.

During the process, be sure to involve all concerned departments like Corporate Communications, Human Resources, Marketing, Facilities Management, Fleet Management, and Purchasing. Different managers are motivated by different things and need to be addressed in different ways. Treat the departments with respect as they are integral to delivering a successful implementation program. Don't forget to communicate the project goals to the people who have to work daily with the brand after the implementation.

10. Don't forget the external communications to relevant stakeholders like customers, media, and shareholders.

A brand implementation is an excellent opportunity to tell the brand story, including the brand positioning and the brand values.

(B)Pricing

2.7 Definition of pricing

Method adopted by a firm to set its selling price. It usually depends on the firm's average costs, and on the customer's perceived value of the product in comparison to his or her perceived value of the competing products.

Different pricing methods place varying degree of emphasis on selection, estimation, and evaluation of costs, comparative analysis, and market situation.

2.8 Some of the more common pricing objectives are:

- maximize long-run profit.
- maximize short-run profit.
- increase sales volume (quantity)
- increase monetary sales.
- increase market share.
- obtain a target rate of return on investment (ROI)
- obtain a target rate of return on sales.

Survival

Prices are flexible. A company can lower them in order to increase sales enough to keep the business going. The company uses a survival-based price objective when it's willing to accept short-term losses for the sake of long-term viability.

Profit

Price has both direct and indirect effects on profit. The direct effect relates to whether the price covers the cost of producing the product. Price affects profit indirectly by influencing how many units sell. The number of products sold also influences profit through economies of scale -- the relative benefit of selling more units. The primary profit-based objective of pricing is to maximize price for long-term profitability.

Related Reading: New-Product Pricing Vs. Market-Penetration Pricing

Sales

Sales-oriented pricing objectives seek to boost volume or market share. A volume increase is measured against a company's own sales across specific time periods. A company's market share measures its sales against the sales of other companies in the industry. Volume and market share are independent of each other, as a change in one doesn't necessarily spur a change in the other.

Status Quo

A status quo price objective is a tactical goal that encourages competition on factors other than price. It focuses on maintaining market share, for example, but not increasing it, or matching a competitor's price rather than beating it. Status quo pricing can have a stabilizing effect on demand for a company's products.

2.9 Factors Affecting Pricing Product:

A. Internal Factors:

1. Cost:

While fixing the prices of a product, the firm should consider the cost involved in producing the product. This cost includes both the variable and fixed costs. Thus, while fixing the prices, the firm must be able to recover both the variable and fixed costs.

2. The predetermined objectives:

While fixing the prices of the product, the marketer should consider the objectives of the firm. For instance, if the objective of a firm is to increase return on INVESTMENT, then it may charge a higher price, and if the objective is to capture a large market share, then it may charge a lower price.

3. Image of the firm:

The price of the product may also be determined on the basis of the image of the firm in the market. For instance, HUL and Procter & Gamble can demand a higher price for their brands, as they enjoy goodwill in the market.

4. Product life cycle:

The stage at which the product is in its product life cycle also affects its price. For instance, during the introductory stage the firm may charge lower price to attract the customers, and during the growth stage, a firm may increase the price.

5. Credit period offered:

The pricing of the product is also affected by the credit period offered by the company. Longer the credit period, higher may be the price, and shorter the credit period, lower may be the price of the product.

6. Promotional activity:

The promotional activity undertaken by the firm also determines the price. If the firm incurs heavy advertising and sales promotion costs, then the pricing of the product shall be kept high in order to recover the cost.

B. External Factors:

1. Competition:

While fixing the price of the product, the firm needs to study the degree of competition in the market. If there is high competition, the prices may be kept low to effectively face the competition, and if competition is low, the prices may be kept high.

2. Consumers:

The marketer should consider various consumer factors while fixing the prices. The consumer factors that must be considered includes the price sensitivity of the buyer, purchasing power, and so on.

3. Government control:

Government rules and regulation must be considered while fixing the prices. In certain products, government may announce administered prices, and therefore the marketer has to consider such regulation while fixing the prices.

4. Economic conditions:

The marketer may also have to consider the economic condition prevailing in the market while fixing the prices. At the time of recession, the consumer may have less money to spend, so the marketer may reduce the prices in order to influence the buying decision of the consumers.

5. Channel intermediaries:

The marketer must consider a number of channel intermediaries and their expectations. The longer the chain of intermediaries, the higher would be the prices of the goods.

Pricing Methods

Cost-plus pricing - Set the price at your production cost, including both cost of goods and fixed costs at your current volume, plus a certain profit margin. For example, your widgets cost Rs.20 in raw materials and production costs, and at current sales volume (or anticipated initial sales volume), your fixed costs come to Rs.30 per unit. Your total cost is Rs.50 per unit. You decide that you want to operate at a 20% markup, so you add Rs.10 (20% x Rs.50) to the cost and come up with a price of Rs.60 per unit. So long as you have your costs calculated correctly and have accurately predicted your sales volume, you will always be operating at a profit.

- **Target return pricing** - Set your price to achieve a target return-on-Investment (ROI). For example, let's use the same situation as above, and assume that you have Rs.10,000 invested in the company. Your expected sales volume is 1,000 units in the first year. You want to recoup all your investment in the first year, so you need to make Rs.10,000 profit on 1,000 units, or Rs.10 profit per unit, giving you again a price of Rs.60 per unit.

Value-based pricing - Price your product based on the value it creates for the customer. This is usually the most profitable form of pricing, if you can achieve it. The most extreme variation on this is "pay for performance" pricing for services, in which you charge on a variable scale according to the results you achieve. Let's say that your widget above saves the typical customer Rs.1,000 a year in, say, energy costs. In that case, Rs.60 seems like a bargain - maybe even *too* cheap. If your product reliably produced that kind of cost savings, you could easily charge Rs.200, Rs.300 or more for it, and customers would gladly pay it, since they would get their money back in a matter of months. However, there is one more major factor that must be considered.

- **Psychological pricing** - Ultimately, you must take into consideration the consumer's perception of your price, figuring things like:

    - **Positioning** - If you want to be the "low-cost leader", you must be priced lower than your competition. If you want to signal high quality, you should probably be priced higher than most of your competition.

    - **Popular price points** - There are certain "price points" (specific prices) at which people become much more willing to buy a certain type of product. For example, "under Rs.100" is a popular price point. "Enough under Rs.20 to be under Rs.20 with sales tax" is another popular price point, because it's "one bill" that people commonly carry.

Meals under Rs.5 are still a popular price point, as are entree or snack items under Rs.1 (notice how many fast-food places have a Rs.0.99 "value menu"). Dropping your price to a popular price point might mean a lower margin, but more than enough increase in sales to offset it.

- **Fair pricing** - Sometimes it simply doesn't matter what the value of the product is, even if you don't have any direct competition. There is simply a limit to what consumers perceive as "fair". If it's obvious that your product only cost Rs.20 to manufacture, even if it delivered Rs.10,000 in value, you'd have a hard time charging two or three thousand dollars for it -- people would just feel like they were being gouged. A little market testing will help you determine the maximum price consumers will perceive as fair.

First Steps

To develop a pricing strategy, the first step is to gather data:

Competitor prices and pricing strategies

Customer perception of products and services

Customer benefits of products and services

Cost of producing, procuring, or generating products and services (variable costs)

Fixed business costs (overhead)

The goal is to understand your business model and operating costs as well as the current pricing strategies and price points in the marketplace.

Basic Pricing Methods

Once you have data in hand, apply one or more pricing methods to the specific business and market:

Cost-Plus: Production costs are determined and then a target profit margin is applied. For example, if a product costs Rs.10 to manufacture, and the business wants to make a 20% profit, the price is Rs.12 per unit.

Targeted Return: Investment costs are determined, and a targeted rate of return is applied to deliver the required return on investment. For example, if investment costs are estimated to be Rs.5 per unit, and investors seek a 10% return on investment, the price is Rs.5.50 per unit.

Value: The value customers receive is calculated and pricing is applied accordingly. For example, if a personal session with a business advisor provides the same value as a two-day seminar, the personal session could be priced at the same level (or higher if individual attention and mentoring provides an even greater value than group-based training).

Psychology: Psychological or emotional impact is used to determine final pricing. For example, customers may respond more positively to a product with a price of Rs.199.00 than to the same product priced at Rs.200.00.

Price Strategy Objectives

Business strategies can also affect price. Keep in mind each strategy can have multiple effects; some positive, some negative. The company may use pricing strategies seeking to:

Maximize Current Profits: Higher prices, at least in the short term, can help improve overall profit margins. Of course, over time high prices may result in significantly fewer transactions and lower revenues.

Maximize Cash Flow: Lower prices can increase transactions and increase overall revenue and boost cash flow – but possibly at the expense of profitability.

Maximize Profit Margins: Higher prices yield higher profit margins, but could affect the quantity of sales.

Maximize Sales Quantity: Lower prices - or product bundles – can increase the total number of items sold and generate discounts or rebates from suppliers or WHOLESALERS.

Pricing strategies should also be tied to company objectives. The following are common business goals and the effect on pricing:

Serve Different Market Segments: "One size fits all" prices can turn away customers at both ends of the demographic scale. For example, if a company sells a maintenance service, a standard monthly fee of Rs.95 may be too high for small customers and too low for customers who want additional services and faster response times. Fixed prices may not be appropriate for every customer; if that is the case, building price tiers could make sense.

Serve Different Market Verticals: A company that sells individual products to retail customers may decide to sell products to government agencies interested in bulk purchases.

Different pricing strategies are necessary to take into account volume sales, delivery costs, and other factors unique to servicing government clients.

Generate New Customers: Flat fee pricing often generates additional customers, especially if a flat fee is perceived as cheaper than a la carte purchases. Subscription and time-based purchase agreements are common ways of generating new customers. Typically a company will create pricing strategies to generate new customers at a low profit margin, and then seek to provide additional services for additional fees.

Create Additional Sales Opportunities: Existing customers – especially satisfied existing customers – are fertile ground for additional purchases. Tiered pricing systems for services, and ancillary or complementary products for existing products are great ways to generate additional revenue per existing customer.

Minimize Credit Sales: Retail sales are based on cash (or credit card) payments on an up-front basis. Service businesses typically bill after at least a portion of those services have been provided, which requires the company to in effect extend credit. Some businesses develop service plans that include up-front deposits or that require up-front payments. For example, most cable companies charge for services ahead of service delivery; the bill delivered on September 15, for instance, may cover the time period running from Oct. 1 to October 31.

Minimize Barriers to Purchase: Time-based pricing can make an initial purchase more attractive. Variable pricing is most often used for products purchased from television direct marketers: "Three easy payments of Rs.29.95 each!" Variable pricing can make an initial purchase more attractive as well: a company could offer a service for a reduced rate for the first three months, with subsequent months charged at a higher rate. The goal in that case is to give a customer incentive to try a service because the price is low, at least in the short term.

Keep in mind the best pricing strategies are flexible and allow a company to respond to changes in supply or demand, new competition, changes in technology, etc. Price strategies should constantly be evaluated and tested to ensure the company maximizes return on sales while meeting a variety of other goals and needs.

(C) Advertising

2.10 Definition of advertising

Advertising is a form of marketing communication used to persuade an audience to take or continue some action, usually with respect to a commercial offering, or political or ideological support. The activity or profession of producing advertisements for commercial products or services.

Characteristics of an Effective or Persuasive Advertisement

Appealing to Emotions

Persuasion normally requires that you connect with someone's rational or emotional motives in a purchase situation. In many cases, emotional appeals carry more influence. Effective ads typically rely on strong market research to uncover what makes target customers tick, or what benefits and message content will get their intention. Emphasizing the benefits that most appeal to a target audience in a way that makes an emotional impact is a key ingredient. For example, associating a perfume with sensuality can appeal to a potential customer's yearning to be attractive.

Using Subtlety

The most memorable and resonating ads usually walk a

fine line between clarity and subtlety. You want customers to "get" your message, but you also want them to have to think a little bit so you can create some cognitive residue, or lasting impact. This is where the role of creativity becomes important. Companies often use metaphors to depict the benefits of their brand in a slightly unique or different message situation. This forces customers to connect the dots to the point you make, without completely confusing them about your brand. For example, a gum maker's TV ad might associate a cool mint flavor with a brisk, crisp wintry day by releasing an ad showing someone popping the gum into their mouth, then playing a distant wintry-wind sound effect in the background.

Telling a Story

Effective ads can tell stories to connect with customers, often creating settings with characters that can cause the viewer or listener to identify with a character's plight in the ad. For instance, an ad for auto insurance might depict a driver getting into a fender bender and experiencing the frustration of not having adequate auto coverage. Potential customers might relate, either because they have been in this predicament or can imagine the stress they would feel if they were.

The Medium and the Message

Effective and persuasive ads are delivered in the right way through the right medium. In a TV ad, setting, lighting, sound, character expressions and dialogue all contribute to the mood of the message. In print ads, the design, use of color and copy impact tone. On the radio, the blend of sound and copy set the tone. The medium and message should work together for clarity and impact. Commercials for cologne or perfume often use sensual music, lighting and character gestures to convey messages that the brand offers an attractive, alluring smell.

2.11 Objectives of Advertising

Four main Objectives of advertising are:

i. Trial

ii. Continuity

iii. Brand switch

iv. Switching back

Let's take a look on these various types of objectives.

1. **Trial:** the companies which are in their introduction

stage generally work for this objective. The trial objective is the one which involves convincing the customers to buy the new product introduced in the market. Here, the advertisers use flashy and attractive ads to make customers take a look on the products and purchase for trials.

2. **Continuity:** this objective is concerned about keeping the existing customers to stick on to the product. The advertisers here generally keep on bringing something new in the product and the advertisement so that the existing customers keep buying their products.

3. **Brand switch:** this objective is basically for those companies who want to attract the customers of the competitors. Here, the advertisers try to convince the customers to switch from the existing brand they are using to their product.

4. **Switching back:** this objective is for the companies who want their previous customers back, who have switched to their competitors. The advertisers use different ways to attract the customers back like discount sale, new advertise, some reworking done on packaging, etc.

2.12 Importance of Advertising

1. Advertising is important for the customers

Just imagine television or a newspaper or a radio channel without an advertisement! No, no one can any day imagine this. Advertising plays a very important role in customers life. Customers are the people who buy the product only after they are made aware of the products available in the market. If the product is not advertised, no customer will come to know what products are available and will not buy the product even if the product was for their benefit. One more thing is that advertising helps people find the best products for themselves, their kids, and their family. When they come to know about the range of products, they are able to compare the products and buy so that they get what they desire after spending their valuable money. Thus, advertising is important for the customers.

2. Advertising is important for the seller and companies producing the products

Yes, advertising plays very important role for the producers and the sellers of the products, because

- Advertising helps increasing sales

- Advertising helps producers or the companies to know their competitors and plan accordingly to meet up the level of competition.

- If any company wants to introduce or launch a new product in the market, advertising will make a ground for the product. Advertising helps making people aware of the new product so that the consumers come and try the product.

- Advertising helps creating goodwill for the company and gains customer loyalty after reaching a mature age.

- The demand for the product keeps on coming with the help of advertising and demand and supply become a never ending process.

3. **Advertising is important for the society**

Advertising helps educating people. There are some social issues also which advertising deals with like child labour, liquor consumption, girl child killing, smoking, family planning education, etc. thus, advertising plays a very important role in society.

2.13 disadvantages:

(1) Adds to Costs:

An organisation has to spend large amount on advertising. It increases the cost of the products. To meet this expenditure, price of the product is raised. No manufacturer pays for the advertising expenses out of his pocket. Advertising, therefore, leads to unnecessary rise in prices. In this reference it is said that advertising costs are passed on to the consumers in the form of high prices.

(2) Undermines Social Values:

Advertisement is a sort of day-dreaming for the people. These days it is taking the people away from reality and into the realm of artificiality. Through its medium people get information about new products.

Only very few products are of any use for them. The brilliance of new products really gets on their nerves. They want to buy them but have no resources at their command. Consequently, they start feeling upset with their present status. Taking it as a social evil, it can be said that advertisement undermines social values.

(3) Confuses the Buyers:

Many a time distorted version of reality is shown in the advertising. Believing in advertising, consumers buy the product. On its use, they feel cheated.

They come to realise later that the information given in the advertisement was something else whereas the actual product was quite different from it. Thus, people lose confidence in advertising because of wrong presentation. In this reference it is said that advertising confuses rather than helps.

(4) Encourages Sale of Inferior Products:

Every manufacturer projects his product as superior one in the advertisement. Therefore, the buyer is unable to decide as to which product is really good.

Consequently, it is difficult to get good quality product even after paying a handsome price for it. If a seller gets good price for some inferior product, it becomes a habit with him. It affects other sellers also. Therefore, it is said that advertisement encourages the sale of inferior products.

(5) Some Advertisement is in Bad Taste:

Many times, foul language and objectionable pictures are used in advertising in order to attract a particular class. They may be insulting to a particular class. It causes decay of social values.

Such kinds of advertising are generally opposed by the people as it hurts their feelings. In this reference it is said that some advertisements are in bad tastes.

2.14 Advertising vs Publicity

Some products appear on the market for only a short while and then one will hear nothing about them anymore. Some have been on the market for years, existing since before one is born. For a business to be successful, it needs to promote its name and products so that people will become aware of them. Some companies achieved the popularity and success that they are now enjoying through years of hard work and persistent use of advertising and publicity to promote their products and name.

Advertising is a communications tool which is used to convince viewers, listeners, or readers to do something about a product, an idea, or a service. It is designed to positively influence people to patronize a product or service.

It is usually a paid announcement or promotion to entice people to notice and patronize a company's product through the use of various media such as radio, television, newspapers, magazines, through fliers, and the Internet.

When a company decides to have an advertisement placed in a certain publication, TV, or radio show, it controls how it is presented on the medium which carries it. It can specify the size, scope, and content of the advertisement containing its product. Since it is a paid promotion, customers view advertisements as questionable. It contains only the information that the company specified which is meant to be beneficial to it and no feedback from customers who have tried it.

Publicity, on the other hand, is the promotion and management of the public's impression towards a subject. It is the process of creating news through sponsorship, exhibitions, staging a debate, organizing a tour of the business, and inventing and presenting an award. Through involvement in these activities, the individual or company's name will be extensively mentioned in the media and attract the attention of people to the individual or for consumers to a company's products and services.

Publicity is usually an unpaid promotion, although a minimal cost is incurred for the materials used in the publicity. However, since it is unpaid, the individual or company has no control over how the material is presented if it is released at all. Since it is featured in a magazine or newspaper, the company's name and products being mentioned by a writer or editor, consumers will see them as a positive feedback about the product and the company. People will believe in the product if somebody else talks about it.

Summary:

1.An advertisement is a communications tool which is used to make people patronize a product while publicity is a communications tool which manages people's impressions about a subject.

2.An advertisement is a paid promotion while publicity is free; an individual or company only has to spend funds on the materials needed.

3.In an advertisement, the company can dictate how the information about it is presented including the content while in publicity, the company has no control over how it is shown if at all.

4.Since it comes from a third party, publicity is viewed as more credible by most consumers in contrast to an advertisement which comes directly from the company.

2.15 Types of Advertising Media

- Television
- Radio
- Print Publications
- Internet
- Direct Mail
- Signage
- Product Placement
- Mobile Devices
- Sponsorships
- Other Media Outlets

As we discussed in the Advertising Trends section in the Advertising tutorial, the number of media outlets will continue to grow as new technologies emerge. Thus, marketers are well advised to continually monitor changes occurring within each media outlet.

Unit-03

Consumer Behaviour & Market Segmentation

Consumer Behaviour:

3.0 Meaning and Definition:

Consumer behaviour is the study of how individual customers, groups or organizations select, buy, use, and dispose ideas, goods, and services to satisfy their needs and wants. It refers to the actions of the consumers in the marketplace and the underlying motives for those actions.

Marketers expect that by understanding what causes the consumers to buy particular goods and services, they will be able to determine—which products are needed in the marketplace, which are obsolete, and how best to present the goods to the consumers.

The study of consumer behaviour assumes that the consumers are actors in the marketplace. The perspective of role theory assumes that consumers play various roles in the marketplace. Starting from the information provider, from the user to the payer and to the disposer, consumers play these roles in the decision process.

The roles also vary in different consumption situations; for example, a mother plays the role of an in fluencer in a child's purchase process, whereas she plays the role of a disposer for the products consumed by the family.

Consumer Behaviour is a branch which deals with the various stages a consumer goes through before purchasing products or services for his end use.

Why do you think an individual buys a product ?

- Need
- Social Status
- Gifting Purpose

Why do you think an individual does not buy a product ?

- No requirement
- Income/Budget/Financial constraints
- Taste

When do you think consumers purchase products ?

- Festive season
- Birthday
- Anniversary
- Marriage or other special occasions

3.1 Imporatants of Consumer Behaviour;

1. Buyer behaviour involves both individual processes

and group processes.

2. **Buyer behaviour is reflected from awareness right through post-purchase evaluation indicating satisfaction or non-satisfaction from purchases.**

3. Buyer behaviour includes communication, purchasing and consumption behaviour.

4. Consumer behaviour is basically social in nature. Hence, social environment plays an important role in shaping buyer behaviour.

5. Buyer behaviour includes both consumer and business buyer behaviour.

3.2 Factor of buying behaviour

Cultural Factors - Culture and societal environment

Culture is crucial when it comes to understanding the needs and behaviors of an individual. Basically, culture is the part of every society and is the important cause of person wants and behavior. The influence of culture on buying behavior varies from country to country therefore marketers have to be very careful in analyzing the culture of different groups, regions or even countries. Throughout his existence, an individual will be influenced by his family, his friends, his cultural environment or society that will teach him values, preferences as well as common behaviors to their own culture. For a brand, it is important to understand and take into account the cultural factors inherent to each market or to each situation in order to adapt its product and its marketing strategy. As these will play a role in the perception, habits, behavior or expectations of consumers. For example, in the West, it is common to invite colleagues or friends at home for a drink or dinner. In Japan, on the contrary, invite someone home does not usually fit into the local customs. It is preferable to do that this kind of outing with friends or colleagues in restaurant.

While if a Japanese offer you a gift, the courtesy is to offer him an equivalent gift in return. McDonald s is a brilliant example of adaptation to the specificities of each culture and each market. Well aware of the importance to have an offer with specific products to meet the needs and tastes of consumers from different cultures, the fastfood giant has for example: a McBaguette in France (with french baguette and Dijon mustard), a Chicken Maharaja Mac and a Masala Grill Chicken in India (with Indian spices) as well as a

Mega Teriyaki Burger (with teriyaki sauce) or Gurakoro (with macaroni gratin and croquettes) in Japan.

Sub-cultures

A society is composed of several sub- cultures in which people can identify. Subcultures are groups of people who share the same values based on a common experience or a similar lifestyle in general. Each culture contains different subcultures such as religions, nationalities, geographic regions, racial groups etc. Marketers can use these groups by segmenting the market into various small portions. For example in recent years, the segment of ethnic cosmetics has greatly expanded. These are products more suited to non-Caucasian populations and to types of skin pigmentation for African, Arab or Indian populations for example. It s a real brand positioning with a well- defined target in a sector that only offered makeup products to a Caucasian target until now (with the exception of niche brands) and was then receiving critics from consumers of different origin. Brands often communicate in different ways, sometimes even create specific products (sometimes without significant intrinsic difference) for the same type of product in order to specifically target an age group, a gender or a specific sub-culture. Consumers are usually more receptive to products and marketing strategies that specifically target them.

Social classes

Social classes are defined as groups more or less homogenous and ranked against each other according to a form of social hierarchy. Even if it s very large groups, we usually find similar values, lifestyles, interests and behaviors in individuals belonging to the same social class. Every society possesses some form of social class which is important to the marketers because the buying behavior of people in a given social class is similar. In this way marketing activities could be tailored according to different social classes. Some studies have also suggested that the social perception of a brand or a retailer is playing a role in the behavior and purchasing decisions of consumers. In addition, the consumer buying behavior may also change according to social class. A consumer from the lower class will be more focused on price. While a shopper from the upper class will be more attracted to elements such as quality, innovation, features, or even the social benefit that he can obtain from the product.

Cultural trends

Cultural trends or Bandwagon effect are defined as trends widely followed by people and which are amplified by their mere popularity and by conformity or compliance with social pressure. The more people follow a trend, the more others will want to follow it. For example, Facebook has become a cultural trend. The social network has widely grew to the point of becoming a must have, especially among young people. It is the same with the growth of the tablet market. Tablets such as i-Pad or Galaxy Tab have become a global cultural trend leading many consumers to buy one.

Social Factors

It includes groups (reference groups, aspirational groups and member groups), family, roles and status. This explains the outside influences of others on our purchase decisions either directly or indirectly. Social factors are among the factors influencing consumer behavior significantly. They fall into three categories: reference groups, family and social roles and status.

Family

The family is maybe the most influencing factor for an individual. It forms an environment of socialization in which an individual will evolve, shape his personality, acquire values. But also develop attitudes and opinions on various subjects such as politics, society, social relations or himself and his desires. Buyer behavior is strongly influenced by the member of a family. Therefore marketers are trying to find the roles and influence of the husband, wife and children. If the buying decision of a particular product is influenced by wife then the marketers will try to target the women in their advertisement. Here we should note that buying roles change with change in consumer lifestyles. For example, if you have never drunk Coke during your childhood and your parents have described it as a product full of sugar and not good for health . There is far less chance that you are going to buy it when you will grow up that someone who drinks Coke since childhood..

Personal factors

It includes such variables as age and lifecycle stage, occupation, economic circumstances, lifestyle (activities, interests, opinions and demographics), personality and self concept. These may explain why our preferences often change as our `situation' changes. Decisions and buying behavior are obviously also influenced by the characteristics of each consumer.

Age and way of life

A consumer does not buy the same products or services at 20 or 70 years. His lifestyle, values, environment, activities, hobbies and consumer habits evolve throughout his life. Age and life-cycle have potential impact on the consumer buying behavior. It is obvious that the consumers change the purchase of goods and services with the passage of time. Family life-cycle consists of different stages such young singles, married couples, unmarried couples etc which help marketers to develop appropriate products for each stage. For example, during his life, a consumer could change his diet from unhealthy products (fast food, ready meals, etc.) to a healthier diet, during mid-life with family before needing to follow a little later a low cholesterol diet to avoid health problems.

The factors influencing the buying decision process may also change. For example, the social value of a brand generally plays a more important role in the decision for a consumer at 25 than at 65 years. The family life cycle of the individual will also have an influence on his values, lifestyles and buying behavior depending whether he s single, in a relationship, in a relationship with kids, etc. as well as the region of the country and the kind of city where he lives (large city, small town, country side, etc.) For a brand or a retailer, it may be interesting to identify, understand, measure and analyze what are the criteria and personal factors that influence the shopping behavior of their customers in order to adapt. For example, it is more than possible that consumers living in New York do not have the same behavior and purchasing habits than the ones in Nebraska. For a retailer, have a deep understanding and adapt to these differences will be a real asset to increase sales.

Lifestyle

The lifestyle of an individual includes all of its activities, interests, values and opinions.

The lifestyle of a consumer will influence on his behavior and purchasing decisions. For example, a consumer with a healthy and balanced lifestyle will prefer to eat organic products and go to specific grocery stores, will do some jogging regularly (and therefore will buy shoes, clothes and specific products), etc.

Personality and self-concept

Personality is the set of traits and specific characteristics of each individual. It is the product of the interaction of psychological and physiological characteristics of the individual and results in constant behaviors. It materializes into some traits such as confidence, sociability, autonomy, charisma, ambition, openness to others, shyness, curiosity, adaptability, etc. While the self- concept is the image that the individual has or would like to have of him and he conveys to his entourage. For example, since its launch, Apple cultivates an image of innovation, creativity, boldness and singularity which is able to attract consumers who identify to these values and who feel valued in their self-concept by buying a product from Apple

Occupation

The occupation of a person has significant impact on his buying behavior. For example a marketing manager of an organization will try to purchase business suits, whereas a low level worker in the same organization will purchase rugged work clothes.

Economic Situation

Consumer economic situation has great influence on his buying behavior. If the income and savings of a customer is high then he will purchase more expensive products. On the other hand, a person with low income and savings will purchase inexpensive products.

Lifestyle

Lifestyle of customers is another import factor affecting the consumer buying behavior. Lifestyle refers to the way a person lives in a society and is expressed by the things in his/her surroundings. It is determined by customer interests, opinions, activities etc and shapes his whole pattern of acting and interacting in the world.

Personality

Personality changes from person to person, time to time and place to place. Therefore it can greatly influence the buying behavior of customers. Actually, Personality is not what one wears; rather it is the totality of behavior of a man in different circumstances. It has different characteristics such as: dominance, aggressiveness, self-confidence etc which can be useful to determine the consumer behavior for particular product or service.

Pschological factors

It affecting our purchase decision includes motivation (Maslow's hierarchy of needs), perception, learning, beliefs and attitudes. Other people often influence a consumer s purchase decision. The marketer needs to know which people are involved in the buying decision and what role each person plays, so that marketing strategies can also be aimed at these people. Among the factors influencing consumer behavior, psychological factors can be divided into 4 categories: motivation, perception, learning as well as beliefs and attitudes. Motivation

Motivation is what will drive consumers to develop a purchasing behavior. It is the expression of a need is which became pressing enough to lead the consumer to want to satisfy it. It is usually working at a subconscious level and is often difficult to measure. The level of motivation also affects the buying behavior of customers. Every person has different needs such as physiological needs, biological needs, social needs etc. The nature of the needs is that, some of them are most pressing while others are least pressing. Therefore a need becomes a motive when it is more pressing to direct the person to seek satisfaction. Motivation is directly related to the need and is expressed in the same type of classification as defined in the stages of the consumer buying decision process. To increase sales and encourage consumers to purchase, brands should try to create, make conscious or reinforce a need in the consumer s mind so that he develops a purchase motivation. He will be much more interested in considering and buy their products. They must also, according to research, the type of product they sell and the consumers they target, pick out the motivation and the need to which their product respond in order to make them appear as the solution to the consumers need.

Perception

Perception is the process through which an individual selects, organizes and interprets the information he receives in order to do something that makes sense. The perception of a situation at a given time may decide if and how the person will act. Selecting, organizing and interpreting information in a way to produce a meaningful experience of the world is called perception. There are three different perceptual processes which are selective attention, selective distortion and selective retention. In case of selective attention, marketers try to attract the customer attention. Whereas, in case of selective distortion, customers try to interpret the information in a way that will support what the customers already believe.

Learning

Learning is through action. When we act, we learn. It implies a change in the behavior resulting from the experience. The learning changes the behavior of an individual as he acquires information and experience. For example, if you are sick after drinking milk, you had a negative experience, you associate the milk with this state of discomfort and you learn that you should not drink milk. Therefore, you don t buy milk anymore. Rather, if you had a good experience with the product, you will have much more desire to buy it again next time. The learning theories can be used in marketing by brands.

Beliefs and attitudes

A belief is a conviction that an individual has on

something. Through the experience he acquires, his learning and his external influences (family, friends, etc..), he will develop beliefs that will influence his buying behavior. Customer possesses specific belief and attitude towards various products. Since such beliefs and attitudes make up brand image and affect consumer buying behavior therefore marketers are interested in them. Marketers can change the beliefs and attitudes of customers by launching special campaigns in this regard. To change the brand s marketing message or adjust its positioning in order to get consumers to change their brand perception.

Selective Attention:

The individual focuses only on a few details or stimulus to which he is subjected. The type of information or stimuli to which an individual is more sensitive depends on the person. For brands and advertisers successfully capture and retain the attention of consumers is increasingly difficult. For example, many users no longer pay any attention, unconsciously, to banner ads on the Internet. This kind of process is called Banner Blindness. The attention level also varies depending on the activity of the individual and the number of other stimuli in the environment. For example, an individual who is bored during a subway trip will be much more attentive to a new ad displayed in the tube. It is a new stimuli that breaks the trip routine for him. Consumers will also be much more attentive to stimuli related to a need. For example, a consumer who wishes to buy a new car will pay more attention to car manufacturers ads. While neglecting those for computers. Lastly, people are more likely to be attentive to stimuli that are new or out of the ordinary. For example, an innovative advertising or a marketing message widely different from its competitors is more likely to be remembered by consumers.

Selective Distortion:

In many situations, two people are not going to interpret an information or a stimulus in the same way. Each individual will have a different perception based on his experience, state of mind, beliefs and attitudes. Selective distortion leads people to interpret situations in order to make them consistent with their beliefs and values. For brands, it means that the message they communicate will never be perceived exactly in the same way by consumers. And that everyone may have a different perception of it. That s why it s important to regularly ask consumers in order to know their actual brand perception. Selective distortion often benefits to strong and popular brands. Studies have shown that the perception and brand image plays a key role in the way consumers perceived and judged the product. Several experiments have shown that even if we give them the same product, consumers find that the product is or tastes better when they ve been told that it s from a brand they like than when they ve been told it s a generic brand.

Selective Retention:

People do not retain all the information and stimuli they have been exposed to. Selective retention means what the individual will store and retain from a given situation or a particular stimulus. As for selective distortion, individuals tend to memorize information that will fit with their existing beliefs and perceptions. For example, consumers will remember especially the benefits of a brand or product they like and will forget the drawbacks or competing products advantages.

3.3 The stages of the Buyer Decision Process

The process has been interpreted by many scholars over

the years; however, the five stages framework remains a good way to evaluate the customer's buying process. John Dewey first introduced the following five stages in 1910:

1. **Problem/Need Recognition** This is often identified as the first and most important step in the Customer's Decision Process. A purchase cannot take place without the recognition of the need. The need may have been triggered by internal stimuli (such as hunger or thirst) or external stimuli (such as advertising or word of mouth).

2. **Information Search** Having recognised a problem or need, the next step a customer may take is the Information Search stage, in order to find out what they feel is the best solution. This is the buyer's effort to search internal and external business environments, in order to identify and evaluate information sources related to the central buying decision. Your customer may rely on print, visual, online media or word of mouth for obtaining information.

3. **Evaluation of Alternatives** As you might expect, consumers will evaluate different products or brands at this stage on the basis of alternative product attributes – those

which have the ability to deliver the benefits the customer is seeking. A factor that heavily influences this stage is the customer's attitude. Involvement is another factor that influences the evaluation process. For example, if the customer's attitude is positive and involvement is high, then they will evaluate a number of companies or brands; but if it is low, only one company or brand will be evaluated.

4. Purchase Decision The penultimate stage is where the purchase takes place. Philip Kotler (2009) states that the final purchase decision may be 'disrupted' by two factors: negative feedback from other customers and the level of motivation to accept the feedback. For example, having gone through the previous three stages, a customer chooses to buy a new telescope. However, because his very good friend, a keen astronomer, gives him negative feedback, he will then be bound to change his preference. Furthermore, the decision may be disrupted due to unforeseen situations such as a sudden job loss or relocation.

5. Post-Purchase Behaviour In brief, customers will compare products with their previous expectations and will be either satisfied or dissatisfied. Therefore, these stages are critical in retaining customers. This can greatly affect the decision process for similar purchases from the same company in the future, having a knock-on effect at the Information Search stage and Evaluation of Alternatives stage. If your customer is satisfied, this will result in brand loyalty, and the Information Search and Evaluation of Alternative stages will often be fast-tracked or skipped altogether. On the basis of being either satisfied or dissatisfied, it is common for customers to distribute their positive or negative feedback about the product. This may be through reviews on website, social media networks or word of mouth. Companies should be very careful to create positive post-purchase communication, in order to engage customers and make the process as efficient as possible.

MARKET SEGMENTATION

3.4 Defination:

- Market segmentation is a marketing concept which divides the complete market set up into smaller subsets comprising of consumers with a similar taste, demand and preference.

- A market segment is a small unit within a large market

comprising of like minded individuals.

- One market segment is totally distinct from the other segment.

- A market segment comprises of individuals who think on the same lines and have similar interests.

- The individuals from the same segment respond in a similar way to the fluctuations in the market.

Basis of Market Segmentation

- ### Gender

  The marketers divide the market into smaller segments based on gender. Both men and women have different interests and preferences, and thus the need for segmentation.

  Organizations need to have different marketing strategies for men which would obviously not work in case of females.

  A woman would not purchase a product meant for males and vice a versa.

  The segmentation of the market as per the gender is important in many industries like cosmetics, footwear, jewellery and apparel industries.

- **Age Group**

Division on the basis of age group of the target audience is also one of the ways of MARKET segmentation.

The products and marketing strategies for teenagers would obviously be different than kids.

Age group (0 - 10 years) - Toys, Nappies, Baby Food, Prams

Age Group (10 - 20 years) - Toys, Apparels, Books, School Bags

Age group (20 years and above) - Cosmetics, Anti-Ageing Products, Magazines, apparels and so on

- **Income**

Marketers divide the consumers into small segments as per their income. Individuals are classified into segments according to their monthly earnings.

The three categories are:

High income Group

Mid Income Group

Low Income Group

Stores catering to the higher income group would have different range of products and strategies as compared to stores which target the lower income group.

Pantaloon, Carrefour, Shopper's stop target the high income group as compared to Vishal Retail, Reliance Retail or Big bazaar who cater to the individuals belonging to the lower income segment.

- **Marital Status**

  MARKET segmentation can also be as per the marital status of the individuals. Travel agencies would not have similar holiday packages for bachelors and married couples.

- **Occupation**

  Office goers would have different needs as compared to school / college students.

  A beach house shirt or a funky T Shirt would have no takers in a Zodiac Store as it caters specifically to the professionals.

3.5 Types of Market Segmentation

- **Psychographic segmentation**

  The basis of such segmentation is the lifestyle of the individuals. The individual's attitude, interest, value help the marketers to classify them into small groups.

- **Behaviouralistic Segmentation**

  The loyalties of the customers towards a particular brand help the marketers to classify them into smaller groups, each group comprising of individuals loyal towards a particular brand.

- **Geographic Segmentation**

  Geographic segmentation refers to the classification of market into various geographical areas. A marketer can't have similar strategies for individuals living at different places.

  Nestle promotes Nescafe all through the year in cold states of the country as compared to places which have well defined summer and winter season.

  McDonald's in India does not sell beef products as it is strictly against the religious beliefs of the countrymen, whereas McDonald's in US freely sells and promotes beef products.

3.6 Advantages of Segmentation

There are several advantages of segmentation.

1) Focus of the Company – Segmentation is an effective method to increase the focus of a firm on market segments. If you have better focus, obviously you will have better returns. Numerous automobile companies have started focusing on small car segments. This is nothing else but a company changing its focus for better returns. Thus companies base their strategy completely on a new segment which increases its focus and profitability.

2) Increase in competitiveness – Naturally, once your focus increases, your competitiveness in that market segment will increase. If you are focusing on youngsters, your brand recall and equity with youngsters will be very high. Your market share might increase and the chances of a new competitor entering might be low. The brand loyalty will definitely increase. Thus market segmentation also increases competitiveness of a firm from a holistic view.

3) Market expansion – Geographic segmentation is one type of segmentation where expansion is immediately possible. If you have your market strategy on the basis of grography, then once you are catering to a particular territory, you can immediately expand to a nearby territory. In the same way, if you are targeting customers based on their demography (Ex – reebok targets fitness enthusiasts) then you can expand in similar products (Ex – reebok expanding with its fitness range of clothes and accessories). Segmentation plays a crucial role in expansion. You cannot expand in a territory when you have no idea of which segment of customers you will be meeting.

4) Customer retention – By using segmentation, Customer retention can be encouraged through the life cycle of a customer. The best example of this is the Automobile and the Airlines segment. You will find major example of customer life cycle segmentation in the Hospitality segment whether they be hotels airlines, or hospitals. In India, Titan is an example of products which are planned through the life cycle of a customer. From fast track to Sonata and the high range watches, Titan has them by price segment as well as life cycle segment. Thus a watch is available for any customer who enters a Titan showroom, whatever be his age.

5) Have better communication – One of the factors of marketing mix which is absolutely dependent on STP is Promotions or communications. The communications of a company needs to be spot on for its TARGET market. Thus if you need a target market, you need segmentation.

Communication cannot be possible without knowing your target market. Imagine if you had to make someone across a curtain understand what is politics. You would go on about ruling parties, states, countries and politicians. And when the curtain is taken aside, you find that the person across the curtain is a 5 year old kid. Is there any use talking to him about politics? This shows why communication needs segmentation. If you dont know your market segment, what is their demography, what is their psychology, where they are from, then how can you form a communication message.

6) Increases profitability – Segmentation increases competitiveness, brand recall, brand equity, customer retention, communications. Thus if it is affecting so many factors of your business, then definitely it affects the profitability of the firm. Do you ever see people negotiating in a Nike, Gucci or BMW showrooms? You want. One of the USP's of these brand is their segmentation. They are in fact targeting segments which have no need of bargaining or negotiation. Thus their profitability is high.

Limitations of segmentation

Segmentation also has its limitations as it needs to be

implemented in the proper manner. As segmentation is one of the most important process in the marketing plan or for your business, you need to know the limitations of segmentation and what pitfalls lie ahead if you go wrong with your target market segment.

1) **Segments are too small** – If the chosen segment is too small then you will not have the proper turnover which in turn will affect the total margins and the viability of the business.

2) **Consumers are misinterpreted** – The right product to the wrong customers. What if your market research says that your customers want a new soap and you come out with a new facial cream. The concept is same, cleanliness. But the concept is completely different.

3) **Costing is not taken into consideration** – Targeting a segment is ok but you also need to know how much you will have to spend to target a particular segment. If it is a Sec A segment and you do not have the budget to be present in the places the the Sec A customer visits, then your segmentation strategy is a failure.

4) **There are too many brands** – Along with segmentation, you also need to check out the competition offered in the

same segment from other products. Getting into a segment already saturated will mean higher costs and lesser profit margins.

5) **Consumer are confused** – If the consumer himself doesn't know whether he will be interested in a particular product or not, than that's a sign that you need to get out of that segment / product.

6) **Product is completely new** – If a product is completely new than there is no market research to base your segmentation on. You need to market it to the masses and as acceptance increases, only then will you be able to focus on one particular segment.

Unit 04

Market Research

4.0 Introduction to Marketing Research

Market research and marketing **research** are often confused. *'Market'* research is simply research into a specific market. It is a very narrow concept.

'Marketing' research is much broader. It not only includes 'market' research, but also areas such as research into new products, or modes of distribution such as via the Internet.

"Marketing research is the function that links the consumer, customer, and public to the marketer through information – information used to identify and define marketing opportunities and problems; generate, refine, and evaluate marketing actions; monitor marketing performance; and improve understanding of marketing as a process. Marketing research specifies the information required to address these issues, designs the methods for collecting information, manages and implements the data collection process, analyzes, and communicates the findings and their implications."

4.1 Objectives of Marketing Research:

Marketing research is undertaken for attaining the following objectives:

(1) To Provide Basis For Proper Planning:

Marketing and sales forecast research provides sound basis for the formulation of all marketing plans, policies, programmes and procedures.

(2) To Reduce Marketing Costs:

Marketing research provides ways and means to reduce marketing costs like selling, advertisement and distribution etc.

(3) To Find Out New Markets for The Product:

Marketing research aims at exploring new markets for the product and maintaining the existing ones.

(4) To Determine Proper Price Policy:

Marketing research is considered helpful in the formulation of proper price policy with regard to the products.

(5) To Study in Detail Likes and Dislikes of the Consumers:

Marketing research tries to find out what the consumers, (the men and women who constitute the market) think and want. It keeps us in touch with the consumers, minds and to study their likes and dislikes.

(6) To Know The Market Competition:

Marketing research also aims at knowing the quantum of competition prevalent in the market about the product in question. The company may need reliable information about competitor's moves and strategies which are of immense significance for further planning.

(7) To Study The External Forces and Their Impact:

Marketing research provides valuable information by studying the impact of external forces on the organisation. External forces may include conditions developing in foreign markets, govt, policies and regulations, consumer incomes and spending habits, new products entering in the market and their impact on the company's products.

4.2 Scope Marketing Research

the following scope was identified for the project team:

- Identify between four and eight industry sectors (one per WD region and up to four pan-west or multi-region) that have either a recognized global competitive advantage or prospects of such an advantage.

- Articulate the business case advantages (including, but

not limited to, location, transportation, infrastructure, availability of labour, cost of doing business and level of engagement in global supply chains) currently enjoyed by each of the identified sectors.

- Provide intelligence on tools, strategies and policies that would stimulate value-added activities, foreign direct investment (FDI) and small- and medium-enterprise (SME) involvement in these sectors.

- Provide information on best practice examples from five regions or countries that show how the government and private sector work together through economic programs, regulations and/or policies that improve the competitiveness, attractiveness to foreign direct investment and opportunity for economic growth through value-added activity that could apply to the western Canadian context.

4.3 Advantages of Marketing Research:

Importance:

The following advantages offered by marketing research show its importance:

1. Facilitates planned production:

By forecasts of probable sales in the coming years.

2. Discovery of causes of consumer's resistance:

It helps in identifying the reasons for consumer resistance to existing or new products.

3. Correction of defects:

It reveals defects and therefore makes corrective action possible.

4. Reveals the nature of demand:

It brings out whether the product is in constant demand throughout the year or has a seasonal demand.

5. Effectiveness of existing channels of distribution:

For example, in the case of TVs it may be discovered that after sale service is not satisfactory. Then, arrangements may be made to remove such grievances of the customers.

6. Product utility:

It indicates why exactly the product is being purchased by the people and what exact service do they get out of it. For example, a market research conducted by Hindustan Lever Ltd., revealed that their 'Sunlight Soap' which was originally intended to serve as a washing soap, was being used as toilet soap by many people.

7. New uses of the product:

Marketing research may reveal certain new uses for the existing products.

8. Market **information**:

It provides complete information about the market and the changes that are likely to occur in demand for a certain product.

9. Discovery of potential market:

It provides information about the possibility of potential (future) market.

10. Discovery of new lines of production:

It helps in the discovery of supplementary lines of products.

Limitations of Marketing Research:

It is important to note here the following limitations of market research:

(i) A research study will fail to serve its purpose if marketing researcher merely collects some statistical facts; or is preoccupied with techniques or; uses data of questionable validity; or communicates the findings in too much vague or technical language.

(ii) A research study will suffer if the marketing manager does not offer full perspective of the research problem; or allows inadequate time; or uses research as a 'fire-fighting' device; or does not really appreciate the value of research.

(iii) Marketing research cannot by itself provide the solution or make the decision. It only reveals relevant information to the marketing managers who can be able then to make sound and strategic marketing decisions.

4.4 The Marketing research Process.

Marketing research is gathered using a systematic approach. An example of one follows:

1. Define the problem. Never conduct research for things that you would 'like' to know. Make sure that you really 'need' to know something. The problem then becomes the focus of the research. For example, why are sales falling in New Zealand?

2. How will you collect the data that you will analyze to solve your problem? Do we conduct a telephone survey, or do we arrange a focus group? The methods of data collection will be discussed in more detail later.

3. Select a sampling method. Do we us a random sample, stratified sample, or cluster sample?

4. How will we analyze any data collected? What software will we use? What degree of accuracy is required?

5. Decide upon a budget and a timeframe.

6. Go back and speak to the managers or clients requesting the research. Make sure that you agree on the problem! If you gain approval, then move on to step seven.

7. Go ahead and collect the data.

8. Conduct the analysis of the data.

9. Check for errors. It is not uncommon to find errors in sampling, data collection method, or analytic mistakes.

10. Write your final report. This will contain charts, tables, and diagrams that will communicate the results of the research, and hopefully lead to a solution to your problem. Watch out for errors in interpretation.

4.5 Marketing Research V/S Market Research:

Marketing research is a broader term including market research. Marketing research is concerned with all the major functions of marketing. Market research is primarily concerned with knowing the capacity of the market to absorb a particular product. Marketing research is not only concerned with the jurisdiction of the market but also covers nature of the market, product analysis, sales analysis, time, place and media of advertising, personal selling and marketing intermediaries and their relationships etc.

Secondary Market Research and Data

Secondary data is the data collected by someone else other than the researcher himself. This data can be gathered from government records, books, Trade associations, national or international institutes, statistics agencies, etc. Research done using this readily available information is called Secondary market Research.

Factors to be considered while collecting data from secondary sources :

1) Accuracy of data: One should evaluate the credibility of source of data and methods used to collect data because these factors directly influence the accuracy of data.

2) Time and Cost required to collect data: Some sources of data charge money in order to give access to their information, so an organization needs to evaluate this cost with the cost of collecting data by themselves (primary market research).

3) One also needs to take care that information collected

answers the issues which need to be addressed.

Advantages of Secondary Market Research

1) **Time and Cost effective :** Usually time and cost required to collect secondary data is less than efforts required to collect primary data. Data is available freely or at far lesser cost through secondary sources.

2) **Extensiveness of data :** Data collected by governments and other institutes is usually very extensive and covers a large spectrum of issues. An organization can filter that data and consider only parts which they are targeting.

3) **Basis of Primary Research :** Data collected from secondary sources gives an idea to organization about effectiveness of primary research. From secondary data one can form hypothesis and can evaluate the cost and efforts required to conduct own surveys. One can also note down issues, which are not covered from secondary research and, need to be addressed through primary research.

Disadvantages of Secondary Market Research

1) **Data Definitions :** Secondary Researcher needs to understand various parameters and assumptions that primary research had taken while collected information. A term may

have different meaning for different people, example a term 'youth' used is ambiguous and one needs to find what is the assumed age taken by primary researcher.

2) **Inaccuracy of Data :** As we are not gathering our own information, first-hand, we are totally dependent on someone else's efforts. Primary researcher may have been biased or may have used questionable methods to collect data; this can be pretty risky for secondary researchers to base their report on such data.

3) **Time Lag Issues:** Information collected from books, historical surveys are usually not sync with the times and might have changed drastically. Thus making such information a foundation of research may be highly risky for the business or project.

4) **May not be Specific :** Extensiveness of such information is its benefit as well as drawback. Organization will not get answers to their specific issues through this data directly and one needs to 'mine' further into it to get relevant information.

5) **Proprietary Issues :** Some of the secondary sources might have copyrighted their information and using them without permission can lead to various legal complications.